TO MY
BRAVE
COUNTRYMEN

CHRISTOPHER PHILLIP

authorHOUSE®

AuthorHouse™
1663 Liberty Drive
Bloomington, IN 47403
www.authorhouse.com
Phone: 833-262-8899

Published by AuthorHouse 09/25/2021

ISBN: 978-1-6655-3669-1 (sc)
ISBN: 978-1-6655-3668-4 (e)

Library of Congress Control Number: 2021917858

Print information available on the last page.

Any people depicted in stock imagery provided by Getty Images are models, and such images are being used for illustrative purposes only.
Certain stock imagery © Getty Images.

This book is printed on acid-free paper.

To My Brave Countrymen

The strengths of liberty

Within democracy

Descends from dignity

Crowning each citizen

With humble equality

Regardless of origin

Or gender or creed,

For such is decency.

Within this unsure world we find ourselves grasping onto the sanctity of life, mere steps away from death. As we rise to forge our survival, our very being is centered on life and its necessaries. And we celebrate life. For if we worshipped death, would we not be hypocrites? Therefore, we uphold and protect life. Yet as history has shown us, there are some who wish to destroy. Thus one might say, "Who has made thee god that thou should take away that which hast been divinely given?" Yet more must act to protect those who cannot protect themselves. This, I posit, is the most basic definition of society—the protection of those who cannot protect themselves. Hence, every just law protects oneself from death. Lo, there are many types of death, but that is another subject. Let us today speak of life.

The noblest have always upheld the sanctity of life within our world. Yet history is laden with horrific accounts of countless wars, murders, and betrayals that some nations must undergo to secure a ruler. And if rulers obtain their powers through evil, how will their disposition be? It is very noble indeed, in a fair and ordered manner, to peacefully elect representatives by the majority of an electoral college to serve the will of the people. The very concept of a democracy governing by the consent of the people through separate balanced powers is intended to protect a society against tyrannical dictators. Blessed are the fountains of democracy that bring forth the sweet waters of liberty, bestowing equality to all who drink. Let us protect these waters accordingly.

Our forefathers, who had been loyal subjects of the Crown, knew that evil could spring from the best intentions. Therefore, our founders, when establishing the powers of our democratic republic, secured the rights of the individual citizen in order to form a more perfect union. Was not one who was considered wise quoted as saying, "Is it not better for one man to die, than for a whole nation to perish?" Alas, did not the nation perish within a generation? In human endeavors, if the ends justify the means, there is no reason for a lawgiver. Yet if the means determine the ends, then securing the rights of the individual secures the right for a government to govern.

The supreme law of our land, the Constitution of the United States of America, institutes our democratic republic. With the purpose of establishing justice, ensuring domestic tranquility, providing common defense, promoting the general welfare, and securing the blessings of liberty, the Constitution forms a more perfect union. Let us remember that *we the people of the United States* have formed this union. It is only by the consent of the people that a government can govern. Our American government was formed to secure life, liberty, and the pursuit of happiness. Therefore, our elected representatives swear to uphold and protect our American liberties, secured by the Constitution, to ensure our freedom. The right of freedom, so precious and delicate, purchased through great sacrifice, struggles every day against many subjugations. Let us be careful as to what we make ourselves slaves unto.

The founders of America so strongly believed that all men are created equal and endowed with certain inalienable rights of life that they determined to fight for such liberties unto death. Dreams of a more perfect society became an American reality by the daily sacrifices our forefathers deliberately made. Henceforth, certain inalienable rights are secured by the Constitution for every citizen of the United States of America.

Lest I forget the blood of my ancestors shed for my daily liberties, I shall recount these rights as long as I live. The right of religious freedom within the land has blessed me from the poisons of radicalism. Oh, that I might say, "'tis a liberty." And the law of my country allows different perspectives of truths to be publicly discussed in print. Patriots have secured my American liberty to peacefully assemble and petition. The right of the people to keep and bear arms shall not be infringed upon. Also, no American soldier shall be quartered unwillingly with any American citizen. In order to prevent my government from becoming tyrannical, citizens are protected from undue search and seizures.

Against despotism, that I might not be considered a hypocrite among my countrymen, may the limits of criminal trials never taint the weights of blind justice. These limits include grand juries, double jeopardy, speedy trails, public disclosure of charges, jury by peers, defense by counsel, and reserving the right not to testify against oneself. To spare Americans from many evils, cruel and unusual punishment has been forbidden under the Constitution. May I be reminded that the United States is a federation delegating powers through the Constitution by the consent of the states and the people as decreed by our ninth American liberty. Thereby, the Tenth Amendment declares constitutional rights and liberties not explicitly stated may be reserved by future American generations if so prudent.

I will always remember these first ten liberties of the Constitution of the United States were submitted to the states on September 25, 1789, and ratified on December 15, 1791, collectively as the Bill of Rights. The remaining seventeen rights were ratified later to amend the Constitution.

Therefore, the Eleventh Amendment iterates that all of the states of the union are sovereign in a foundation of immunity from foreign powers. Defined election procedures for the President of the United States are explained in the Twelfth Amendment. The thirteenth Constitutional liberty abolishes all from the iniquity of slavery. The definition of citizenship along with the framework of due process, equal protection, and the protection of privileges and immunities is legislated by the ratification of the Fourteenth Amendment. Suffrage is granted for all races of men in our fifteenth American liberty. Congress shall have power to lay and collect taxes. The election of senators is mandated by popular vote in the Seventeenth Amendment. Alcohol was prohibited under the Eighteenth Amendment. The nineteenth American liberty grants suffrage for women.

Let there be a voting schedule, lest everyone be elected in the same season. The Twenty-First Amendment repeals the prohibition of alcohol. To prevent a monarchy, may there be presidential term limits as defined in our Twenty-Second Amendment. Also mandated is that the District of Columbia's presidential electoral votes are equal to the state with the least presidential electoral votes. The twenty-fourth Constitutional liberty forbids poll taxes. To ensure continuity of leadership if there be an absence, the Twenty-Fifth Amendment outlines a proper and orderly succession to the presidency. All citizens eighteen years of age and older in America have-s been granted the right to vote under our wenty-sixth liberty. And last, the Twenty-Seventh Amendment of the Constitution states that congressional salary changes must take place on the next election term of the representatives.

Now that we have named the rights of our nation, we must understand that as our nation's liberties are derived from the liberties of the individual, so our nation's virtues are also related to the virtues of the individual. Where people are prudent, just, and courageous, so their nation will shine with prudence, justice, and courage. Nations, which lead through the darkness of uncertainty to give direction, must be comprised of people who hold deep convictions about faith, hope, and love. And without question, the greatest feats of humanity have always been accomplished through due diligence to the virtues.

I, too, desire to see in this country that decent men are strong and strong men are decent. Therefore, concerning attributes of strength, truthfulness is the most critical because it is the sum of all the virtues. People base their confidence and hope on what is considered truthful. It is courageous and just to be forthright. Common sense states that honesty is most often prudent. Dignity is free from guile. Love for one another manifests honesty. One readily endures with fortitude when principles taken to heart are truthful. And people often find peace in knowing the truth.

True worth is in being, not in seeming. Insofar that life is a reality to experience, we should hold our experiences in truth, not in deceit, if only for our survival. Over the centuries, has not humanity continually searched for the truth? Our hearts inherently hunger for the essence of truth. Thus society rightly reverences those who tell the truth, for with truth there is duty. Let us not fool ourselves, this is wisdom—to thine own self be true.

If honesty is to be esteemed, we must realize that life must be endured with courage. In both adversity and danger, our spirits must not give up the hope that truth and freedom benefit both the present and future generations. I pray that you might not abandon the duty of preserving the principles that America is founded upon. One must travel up steep inclines in order to arrive at the mountaintop. Let us endure bravely with fortitude in continuing to forge the American dream into reality.

By great sacrifice our forefathers pursued the formation of utopia, that is, a more perfect society than the world had ever witnessed before. And when one tries to perfect, the divine nature of humanity often rises to great heights, casting a shadow of righteousness on all. The Messiah has said that a city is placed on a hill to be seen. Let the world marvel—a society which secures individual liberties while maintaining fair moral and economic conditions is a more perfect society that blesses all people regardless of birth. For when the highest standards of liberty and opportunity are modeled in a society, the yield brings forth a bold character of equality that benefits both the proudest and the most humble.

Societies of the past relied on their rulers for justice. With the advent of democracy, the rule of law has decreed that all are equal and no one is above the law. Blessed are the people who rule themselves with laws that are stronger than their own fleeting passions. Good laws are based on sound virtues. Good laws protect as well as foster trust. Good laws are based on fair judgements. Likewise, bad laws and wrong judgments corrupt relationships and erode trust. The strength of a society is determined by a person's commitment to the ideals of that society. Let us be courageous and faithful in respect to others so that our society might be worthy of ourselves.

Our postmodern society is evolving in complexity as people continue to specialize. With this specialization, societies are becoming more interdependent on one another. As globalization rapidly shrinks our world, networks are being developed throughout the world as people become associated in more unique ways. More than ever, individuals from different cultures and societies are interacting with one another. What might appear to be societal divisions are in actuality only social complexities. Since we all are human, cultures differ only in degrees of complexity not in construct.

Movements of societal complexities prove their existence. These complexities move in many different directions with and against various equilibriums. People often differ in being able to consistently define an equilibrium. The answer is relative, depending on the individual. One might substitute the technical word "equilibrium" with the concept "harmony" for context. I posit that within America our societal harmony is based upon the protection of our individual liberties. The due protection of every American's civil liberties is paramount to secure harmony and stability within our society.

There are some who have come to believe that the government of the people, by the people, and for the people has lost sight of its purpose. Indeed, throughout the centuries, many generations with great sacrifice have undertaken the noble duty of preserving our liberties in adversity. The testimonies of our fathers, mothers, children, brothers, and sisters cry out that our freedoms are purchased by both life and blood. Even though our liberties of freedom struggle against those who are evil, every American must come to realize in postmodern times that we must dedicate ourselves to our conscience and endure. For I am of the strong opinion that the greatest asset that our nation possesses are the very citizens of the United States of America.

Many nations have kings and queens. Some have wondered about my allegiance. My allegiance is not a mystery, for I have pledged my allegiance since I was a child. My king who leads my nation is stained with reverent blood from great sacrifices of men and women who have fought to protect my freedoms against tyranny. My king is of the color of all colors, the innocence of my nation's young who cannot protect themselves. My king is also of the enduring hardworking blue, determined to forge the necessities of life. The king to whom I pledge my allegiance is the flag of the United States of America. Here lies the physical embodiment of the Constitution of the United States, our American flag.

I have spoken of our individual liberties, which I believe make the United States of America great. Ensuring our freedom through a more perfect union, our American liberties have brought forth many blessings. As our ancestors before, let us continue to fight through adversity for liberty. Our very own actions will determine our fate. And it is good to set forth actions that bring forth blessings. Yet there will be times when our actions will bring forth the unexpected. While the unexpected often baffles and mystifies, I believe our American liberties will continue to bless all of our encounters. In my lifetime, I have encountered the unexpected. I know that I have never done the actions of a diviner—I have only sought the counsel of the L-RD G-D of the Most High. Each time I encountered the supernatural, I prayed to G-D. When my computer spoke to me, I prayed only

to G-D. For years I tried to rationalize and minimalize the situation, but I believe that I cannot anymore. When I stand before G-D at the great Throne of Judgment, I am determined to have a clear conscious. I wish to bravely set forth into the future with faith in my nation and G-D.

When arriving upon the unexpected, we must know in our hearts what we hold dear and what makes us great, if we are to be greater than the unexpected.

Of sunsets and sunrises,

As their zenith angles right

Astral fires alight

Under quite the same thrall.

Ever twin phoenixes,

Whether rising or falling

From old death or new birth,

Does not such depend upon?

Our passage going forth.